Rat Romeo

Some of these poems have previously appeared in print:

Accidental Renaissance: *Queen's Quarterly*, Fall 2024.
The Kiss, The Drowning, Calorimetry: *Sanctuary: Cootes Paradise Writers Anthology*, Vol 5, 2024.
Horror Novel, Road Trips and Red Jello, The Murders: *The River*, Winter 2024.
On Losing a War: *Queen's Quarterly*, Winter 2024.
A Five-Act Poem: *The Sandy River Review*, Spring 2024.
The Politics of Violence: *Hidden Peak Review*, Spring 2024.
I'll Take a Short Death Please, Almost Touch, Advice After a Storm, Friend, To the Girl Who Returned My Stolen Guitar: *Pennsylvania Literary Journal*, 2025.
Death On the Tracks: *The River*, Winter 2025.
The Murders: *Sanctuary: Cootes Paradise Writers Anthology*, Vol 6, 2025.
Pinhole Camera, Dorchester Prison, Impersonating Puxley, Pool Hopping: *Exile Quarterly*, 2025.
The Scar: *The Malahat Review*, Spring 2025.
Atlantic Flowers, Job Interview at the Rose & Crown, Charlbury Oxon, Brantford Serenade: *The Queen's Review*, 2025.
Halcyon Days, Trade Union Tire Spikes, Goodbye: *Pennsylvania Literary Journal*, 2026.
Costume Democracy, Donnie is Coming For Sure: *samfifty-four*, Summer 2025.
Public Acclaim at the Liquor Control Board of Ontario: *Queen's Quarterly*, Spring 2026

Rat Romeo

Poems

Gerald Arthur Moore

CANADA

Copyright © 2025 by Gerald Arthur Moore

All rights reserved. No part of this book may be used or reproduced in any manner whatsoever without the prior written permission of the publisher, except in the case of brief quotations embodied in reviews.

Publisher's note: This book is a work of fiction. Names, characters, places and incidents are either the product of the author's imagination or are used fictitiously, and any resemblance to actual persons living or dead is entirely coincidental.

Library and Archives Canada Cataloguing in Publication

Title: Rat romeo : poems / Gerald Arthur Moore.

Names: Moore, Gerald Arthur, 1972- author.

Identifiers: Canadiana 20250227967 | ISBN 9781989689912 (softcover)

Subjects: LCGFT: Poetry.

Classification: LCC PS8626.O5937 R37 2025 | DDC C811/.6—dc23

Printed and bound in Canada on 100% recycled paper.

Now Or Never Publishing
901, 163 Street
Surrey, British Columbia
Canada V4A 9T8

nonpublishing.com
Fighting Words.

We gratefully acknowledge the support of the Canada Council for the Arts and the British Columbia Arts Council for our publishing program.

for Terri

Table of Contents

You know you have had a successful life
if you have as many good friends
as fingers on your right hand.

~ Art's Dad from Ancaster, Ontario

There's a difference between scratching
your ass and tearin' it to pieces.

~ Heather from Monastery, Nova Scotia

I. The East Coast

Schrödinger's Kickstand

A red bicycle sits in liminality on
Schrödinger's kickstand,

lever it up with the rehearsed
confident tap of an instep,

roll out onto assumed July blessings
under the shade of creaking oak,

their eggcorns with Scottish tams that crack
and spiral away from wheels every autumn,

past the dying stand of dry elm. Weave
between the potholes and puddles,

bleed into sidewalk squares, the long concrete
lines with their vanishing points,

the shaggy mane of handlebar tails, spinning
reflectors clipped into spokes,

now tarnished, the dull crimson hue of the
jeweled orb like a setting sun.

This evidence locker still houses her
bicycle after all these years.

Missing is not murdered, but most likely
it is, more likely worse.

For enervative months the parents held out hope,
then, slowly, over the death of days

realized, she was never going to pedal
furiously past in a flourish

then slam into a skid marking their sidewalk
with another crooked rubber grin.

Pinhole Camera

My ingrown toenail was a tulip,
thick with swelling, and blushing
with infection, it radiated like a star.
You took your pinhole camera, set up
for light and shadow,
and memorialized my deformed
homunculus.

When we were trolling
the open-air market in England,
there was a herd of upturned and
gutted deer, fettered by their hooves
at the butchery. You recoiled
into me, and I laughed,
sang, *Do, a deer, a female deer.*
Your eyes were murderous.
I should have taken your hand,
walked you to the pub. Instead,
you stormed off to the Bodleian
to be with your other lovers;
Lord Byron, Sir Walter Raleigh,
Irving Layton.

Back in Canada,
sitting atop a picnic table,
you told me to *take off my armour*
and relax my war face so that we
could fall in love, but I didn't.
A month later, anesthetized with soju,
we made love for the last time,
my foot, throbbing amid our cadence,
that you pressed with bootheel
to feel a surge of something more
than indifference.

Accidental Renaissance

There's a pack of boys above my
classroom door, in their striped
rugby sweaters, all bearing down
on a player as he madly scoops
a loose ball.

We have him trussed like poultry,
hitting the ground,
his face a contortion, bracing
for the impending weight.

Another frame in the triptych has
players in a lineout,
reaching for the heavens
like an ascension fresco,
silhouetted against a blue marble sky.

The last frame is convocation,
the greenery of their youthful faces,
peacocking in burgundy
academic gowns, caps and
tassels, immortals ahead of troubles,
teenagers reading vampire novels,
before laugh lines, before high tides
that dull sharp edges.

In the passing of seasons one was lost
in a motorcycle crash, another
took his father's shotgun, pushed the
trigger with his thumb.

Earlier that day, he called to thank me;
told me about his love for rugby
and how important our team was to him,

and I missed it.

Fringe Pilgrims

Easy squeeze of the clutch lever like
a chrome treble clef, kick it into gear,
oncoming riders, solemn Gothic columns,
give me the low two, tail gunner taps
his half-helmet, bottom rocker outlaw patch
smiles in my rearview,
that hand sign—warning me of heat,
lying in wait, predatorial
in the shadow of our cathedral, wheel
down Saint George Street, ride the
saintly spire past its broad vestibule,
this house of salvation, where a man
froze last winter under an exhaust vent,
a sculpture of suffering, a still life,
where EMTs shoot Naloxone,
shuffling zombies bent backward line up
for methadone, streetwalker crossing
on a long slope to revival, frostbitten stare,
purse strap that she'll tighten like a garrot
to rocket junk, blows me a kiss and spanks
her thigh, pulls up her dress revealing
the tattoo of a gun, she thinks I'm one, pulls it,
points her finger, taking aim, easy on the clutch,
kick it into third, past the delimited pity
of the street advisory committee, the junkies
and their tirades, sex trade carnival barkers,
give throttle, drown them out with my raging
machine, emerge from liminality
to a sun-bleached roadway, kick it into fourth,
free of blistering curb-dirt, glitter glass,
a tickertape parade of syringes, like fan
palm fronds placed by fringe pilgrims.

A Five-Act Poem

Bark with the motorcycle throttle,
and smile at Leah,
she's a ghost wandering the battlements
at midnight. Her junk-sick pimp jumps,
hits the sidewalk, grinding away
with a slouching prison cadence.

Leah slides across a memory box
to stow my Rosary,
an installation art piece
the size of a sparrow with green ribbon,
pasted with tiny porno cutouts
of bare breasted women,
adds for lubricants and XXX offers.
Her eyes are black pools
amidst smudged makeup.
Admits to working a couple
of online prostitution hustles,
turning tricks for crystal
with no Rosencrantz or Guildenstern,
these people all want a piece.

There's a cat-scratch wound
bubbling on her arm that won't heal,
threw high heels in a dumpster behind
the high school,
believed they were conspiring against her,
suspects they are using a tracking chip,
she is Hamlet.

Another job offer—
dancing at Angie's Show Palace,
practicing with a stripper pole
that her boyfriend stole
after he threw her down
a fire escape and left her streetside.
Hands me a journal that wears
the nail polish stink of crack cocaine,
plump with letters, *memento mori* drawings,
some good stanzas,
and at least two poems written in blood.

Is this Shakespeare's fifth act?
Will the players engage in a final duel
with stabbing and poison?
Leah talks—like you and I are talking—
as if everything is peaches,
as if methamphetamine hallucinations
and hard-hat-dives into the sex trade,
as if stolen stripper poles
and penning poems in blood
are all part of the writing process.

Death On the Tracks

Weird-D stepped into the light of a CN locomotive,
eviscerated like a kicked bag of rubber bands

unspooled garden hose, they closed the trainline
all Canada Day and into the dark hours,

his celebration of life marked with yellow Police ribbon,
scraped the rails with ash shovels, polished firetrucks

with mirror chrome wheels hit the tracks with high
pressure water, carrion birds hopped like marionettes,

their shadows freakish in the spinning dance hall lights.
Mortars thumped, spitting cardboard rockets

onto a sky-black canvass; temporary pinwheels
of burning flowers were placed above your grave.

Mourners on the fringes plunged their syringes
during those moments of flashing funerary monuments,

the cortege clatter, the final double thump salute, bright,
sizzled and smoked, into the exhalation of light.

Advice After a Storm

The last rainsquall mauled the modular tent,
pulled corner spikes from our cam-net like tubers,

they skuttled the outdoor mainstage, troubadours
moved indoors to the Canso hockey rink.

We held ground like soldiers in shell scrapes,
danced after hours like early hominids

wheeling around a ceremonial fire, kicking puddles
in huddles when shore winds lashed.

The next morning blushed; crepuscular rays illuminated
silver ellipses being slowly drunken, the ground

completely sodden from a night's bluster. I drank
an entire bottle of wine as a solo project

before those receding pools disappeared, before
the bustling of early birdsong. Heather, from Monastery,

first to rise as if for morwen chores, joining me
for daybreak's glorious gloaming,

remarking on my cockcrow drunkenness,
offered, in her thick East Coast brogue;

"There's a difference between scratching your ass
and tearing it to pieces."

The Wave

Everything was stowed and battened,
bound like hostages. A frigid witch

came shrieking over the deck,
the bow lifted as an arrow to flight,

then sloped into a deep Atlantic swell.
The keel cut water like a scythe,

weightlessness at the wheel,
her life strap taught as a fiddle string.

A stealing shock of saltwater filled the
deck, letting go in the surging chaos,

Wanda whispered to someone
in helpless liberation,

blessed for blood orange skies
and a score of lovers,

came down on her knees, genuflecting
by the gunnel, still tethered.

Dorchester Prison

In 1936, two New Brunswick brothers were simultaneously executed. They were tied back-to-back and hanged.

Razon wire like a spiral notebook spine,
a hopeless hilltop, three story stonework,

somewhere there is hammering, handsaws
are shuffling like stutter steps in jittering

leg irons, a scaffold is being assembled,
two brothers are going to the gallows together,

block turrets, frowning window towers
are picture frames of light and shadow,

this bleak house sings songs of mourning,
lonely etchings in walls feed the dark abyss,

human oils paint every damp railing and brick,
a ghostly chorus of strangulations,

tied back-to-back, the figure-eight-noose
looped infinitely, hands remove spectacles,

their last meal of oyster shells,
their last prayer for an oyster knife.

Renard

We sent strange letters to the President's Lodge,
each about a week apart, signed—Renard.

March 19,
Dear President Starns, We are looking forward
to being your guests in the President's Lodge
for the month of April. Best, best wishes,
Caprice and Renard.

March 25,
Dr. Starns, I'm not sure if you have ever hosted
fowl before, but we don't eat human food;
mostly seeds, algae, grasses, weeds, sometimes
small frogs or fish, we can eat small grains,
such as corn and wheat, you should never feed
us bread; I don't know how that bread thing
got started. Cheers! Caprice and Renard.
PS With these tailwinds we should arrive
by Easter.

March 30,
Dr. Starns, I'm afraid we have been stung
by tragedy. Caprice is gone. She has been killed
by hunters. I will be taking a few days to handle
our affairs, then continuing alone.
Sadly, Renard.

April 3, (Easter Sunday)
A long night of drinking saw the soft liberation
of a mallard from the Halifax Public Gardens.
Renard arrived,
the first college Duck in Residence
at the University of King's College.

Horror Novel

Handsome Mark Sampson is coming,
crossing the Northumberland Strait,
a tanned satchel strapped on his back
like a quiver, plump with pages
from a new novel, chapters that taste
like chilled Prosecco, Picasso piles
of raked leaves to cannonball.

There's an ancient demon temptress
who urges nakedness, to bathe
in moonlight beneath murky waters.
There's a yard sale talisman, a mad
gunman whose Moncton rampage
inspires the arc, a story that wrings
like a twisting bar rag.

You can smell four hundred pages,
images with rancor, heavy odor
on your hands after reading,
like picking pennies off the floor
of a piss-wet washroom. An urge
to wipe-off, for a holy blessing.

Then approach every shadow as
ominous, see specters in bedroom
mirrors and in your nightmares.
Purging his protagonist with
a retching splash, like a teenage
booze-puke behind a camp tent.

Handsome Mark Sampson is
stepping off the boat, the sea breeze
holds a brine. Keep away, keep away
from Lowfield, and your children
within your sightline.

Meeting at 3500 Feet

There were three of us—a magician, a soldier,
and a poet. We practiced our exit from the plane
by jumping from a sick, rickety, picnic table
at the end of a grass airstrip, a swooning striped
windsock slow danced, with a trailer home
doubling as the company office, axle resting
on cinderblocks with chunks of firewood
for wheel chalks. If someone thundered-in,
it looked like the whole skydiving operation
could be dismantled in minutes.

The nine-cell Manta rode my back. I whispered
the emergency procedure like a Rosary,
identify,
grab,
punch right (cut away)
punch left (reserve deploys),
check canopy.

Holding the pilot chute in shaking hands
as if strangling a puppet, its umbilical draped
over my shoulder, pack clinging like a child,
the propeller wound up, a grinding metal cry,
we rumbled down the airstrip. Leaning forward,
resting my head in the jumpmaster's lap
like an apostle. He slid the door open, unwrapped
my murderous hands, took it from my grip,
shouted, *go save your life.* I stepped out, onto a tiny
bicycle pedal strut, wind whipping, unsteady,
tipping. Braced my hands on the frame,
cast a backward glance. The magician and the
soldier tried to signal encouragement, thumbs-up
like goal posts, wearing strange terror smirks.

Reached out for the wing, then dangling,
on his command—released. I fell.
He dropped my pilot chute into the slipstream.
I watched the plane exit stage left,
a storm of turbulence, a crashing constant noise
against my jumpsuit, the reassuring tug,
my main filled with cheeks of air,
billowing taut. The papery land stretched out
with a river crisscrossing the fields, I pulled
the steering toggles down,
heard the satisfying rip of Velcro,
then flared, slowed watched the canopy deflate,
opened the risers again,
began to steer, the dissipation of fear,
knowing there was a magician, overhead,
somewhere.

Pool Hopping

For Marilyn and Scott

We slouch in defilade on a long-curved pew
in Shepody House pouring a sneaky highball,

a century-old church converted to a music venue.
Guitarists strum cat-gut strings, leaning locals

lounge in the south transept, with pocket flasks.
We leave with Risky-Jill the poet.

A blood moon hangs from an unseen wire
in the twilight of our troubles, we travel back

to Moncton, driving the meandering tidal estuary
on the Tantramar Loop for an after-hours fete.

Skulking between houses like cat burglars,
we lower Risky-Jill over a fence,

her Barbie-doll legs able to trip
the latch gate, endless midnight black hair

a detail paintbrush. Like saboteurs, we strip naked
in moonlight, discard our clothes like low cards

slip surreptitious into an inground pool.
Then floodlights and havoc,

our high school principal recognizes us,
lays down his Louisville on a lawn chair

and reels, when, as friendly Nereids,
we emerge in the buff.

To the Girl Who Returned My Stolen Guitar

For ten years I kept the guitar case, a yawning empty sarcophagus.
Me a poet, you, the pawn shop owner's strung-out mistress

who, for payback and a pay cheque, would take me
to the Underworld.

You arrived in a taxi, a red-light Nefertiti, lips stained
with blood ochre, double-winged eyeliner,

peered from five thousand years of childhood fondling,
hard dates, overdose snake cult ceremonies.

Hieroglyphics embellished your long legs, a winged scarab
obscured deeper scars, Eye of Horus,

dangling protective amulets and earrings, difficulty translating
the hieratic medley of symbols and battle histories

carved in stone, a corded bracelet of Duamutef, who will
present you, someday, to the feet of Osirus.

I've included you to my death scroll, my remarkable Nefertiti,
you are sealed, thus preserved, murex words

that celebrate your holiness in the afterlife of this papyrus.
Why did you really steal back my guitar?

Under a pale moon and two radiant stars, we drove
in separate cars, desiccated hearts in canopic jars.

Impersonating Puxley

In an erudite accent,
he'd answer the jet-black rotary dial,
impersonating their old college provost,

"Puxley here."
Later,
falling into a more dramatic Oxonian accent,
with just the right amount of smoker's gravel,

"Puxlaaay-heeyah."

a nonchalant priestly tempo, sermon speed,
singsong sass,

"Puxley,"

'Doing the Pux' became popular on campus.

Eventually,
the inevitable,

a plucked receiver,

"Puxlaaay-heeyah."

a quick beat,
the menacing response,

"Noooo,
Puxley heeeere!"

Eyes alight, mouthing, "Oh no!"
to his roommate,

listening to the other, breathing,

        finally girding his loins,

"Then one of us is lying." And hung up.

Our Friend Wild Bill

My Grade 9 English student,
reluctant reader, interested in truth
and war stories. I wrote to Sergeant
Guarnere, who penned a letter back,
sent Jared a dress uniform photo,
confident, edgy smile, trousers
creased like folded paper,
before his kills, before the blackout
devil's drop into Normandy.

In the house-to-house fighting
of Monte Cassino, his brother Henry,
an army medic, was killed in '44.
Thirsty for Nazi blood, earned
the moniker Wild Bill. Southwest
of Foy, a wood line artillery barrage
shaved off his right leg.

Home in Philly, the fraternal city,
working odd jobs, on rooftops,
tarpaper shingles, hammers and nails,
soldiering-on with crutches or cane
in favour of a prosthetic.

Standing Best Man at Babe Hefron's
wedding, he was a brother,
a Thompson-machine-love-gunner,
imploring Jared, a boy he never
imagined and would never meet,
to read,
to read good books, to value
comradeship, to enjoy school,
and a quiet peace, paid for
by his Easy Company pals.

Wedding Song

Co-written with W.O. Scott MacFarlane

Donnie was rockin', but not to the music,
it seemed the drink had got the best of him,
Willy was dancing with a girl in the corner
while I sat at the table reading Anaïs Nin.

The lads got drinkin' pretty early in the morning,
the day was hot and the beer was for the fight,
young bravado bottled in brown glass bombshells,
danger increased with each round in flight.

Budup-upbup—here's to Paul's wedding,
budup-upbup—I'm on my way,
budup-upbup—here's to Paul's children,
budup-upbup—here's to his fiancée.

Nothing could be faster than the mouth of the Devil,
Shane found out the hard way, as he spoke through his drink,
a guest behind bars, concave floors, no shoelaces,
and his head in the sink.

Budup-upbup—here's to Paul's wedding,
budup-upbup—I'm on my way,
budup-upbup—here's to Paul's children,
budup-upbup—here's to his fiancée.

Willy's girl left him after her twelve-drink limit,
wallets empty and we were late for Mass,
she left with Finley, her pirate lover,
"Last Call," was shouted, Willy said, "Last call my ass."

Budup-upbup—here's to Paul's wedding,
budup-upbup—I'm on my way,
budup-upbup—here's to Paul's children,
budup-upbup—here's to his fiancée.

II. Analepsis

The Scar

All the way round her hip there was an eel
frozen in ice—a long bump protruded from her thigh

from that day she skipped into traffic, a squealing
of shorebird brakes, sliding tires, the gouging metal

edge of an Oldsmobile bumper, her dress soaking
like a full rag, a ribbon of pink skin dangling

like an untied bow. He cradled her to his car, drove
to the hospital himself. That man, visiting from

Baltimore, booked a hotel room in Hamilton,
stayed for days until my mother was out of danger.

As a child, I marveled at the long purple slash
that dipped below her hemline, a cautionary

reminder. In the last days of my mother's sickness
she mentioned him again, told me about the decades

of letters he had penned, until one day they stopped—
handwritten kindnesses, decency resting in a tin box.

Witches' Butter
tremella mesenterica

There's no substance here.
It's growing from dead rot;

a seductively bright jelly
that dares us to touch,

a harvest, disguised as
madness; an orange caterpillar

fresh girl, difficult
to resist, and I taste it

before I can be sure if
it is poisonous.

I Am a Dropped Motorcycle

Bootheel roll over marbles of gravel, awkward
fingers slip from the clutch like sloppy foreplay,

a patellar reflex, nine hundred pounds
of chrome and steel lurch forward, then splay,

a racehorse with a broken leg, lifting her head,
crying out to an indifferent sky and a deaf God.

Dour faced men erect their skeletal frame,
canvas obscura to veil

the *coup de grâce* of the veterinarian.
That's what it is like to love me.

Forgetting

Repainting his grandson, as if to tighten
the tourniquet against a lunatic amputation of

the heart, each canvas a beautiful new agony.
He stirs pigment, creates smooth brown skin

like wet pottery clay, his flat brush moving
over the bony crescent of a fingernail,

tiny hands that he is still holding,
then a tint to gentle eyes

that he never manages to recreate.
After the Haitian earthquake

this old man set up a makeshift easel,
shuffling between cinderblock piles,

reproducing the same face, over and over,
and hawking these portraits to aid workers.

One painting hangs in our own boy's bedroom,
who now asks if the child was in our family.

I am reminded of a carved tablet cartouche
that bears the pharaoh's royal name,

a stone shout into the fearful abyss
of love and forgetting.

Friend

Maria dances from table to table, quick steps,
leans with the coffee urn, keeps your cup alive,
she knows each face and most names,
her elderly father, elbows buttressed against cultured
marble and polished metal, like an old country
taverna patriarch. Across from me, on a restaurant
rumble seat, a girl is crying.

The Dartmouth side's three candy cane smokestacks
pulse like tin ashtrays, chapel resins,
harbour fog incense. The crying girl dries her cheeks
with riotous scarlet hair, a penitent Mary Magdalene
who weeps for Jesus.

Straight from the airport to café cloisters,
kitty corner from Oxford Theatre,
pushes her breakfast around with the leeside
of a fork,—but she knows
his leaving is forever.
A fortnight later, sitting on a gravestone
in The Old Burying Ground on Barrington,
after a bottle of Malbec,
under a gossamer mantle of starlight,
we will kiss because I'm no friend at all.

1989

While she talked to boys, my sister spooled black landline telephone cord around her finger, then she went away to school,

the expanse of attic was mine alone, I celebrated by spinning her forbidden vinyl records on an old turntable.

There was a shooting in Montreal, girls had been the victims because they were girls. If someone called who wasn't my sister,

I said I need to keep this line free and hung up. Icicles drip from the eaves, wrote her name in the frost of a windowpane.

Road Trips and Red Jello (A Song)

Embarking on a road trip
Going to eat some veggie burgers
My girlfriend will do hair wraps
For all of you berserkers
Going to cross Ohio
and Indiana borders
Sharing showers with our girlfriends
Against our parents' orders

Road trips and red jellos along
Road trips and red jellos along

This is not the first road trip
Together we have taken
We avoid the donut shops
And our affinity with bacon
To enjoy the tie dye
And strips down by the seaside
Rainbow colours of balloons
And those with nitrous oxide

Road trips and red jellos along
Road trips and red jellos along

Take the real necessities
Things that cannot be forgotten
A rainbow from your briefcase
And a bowtie made of cotton
Everything else we need
We'll find under the sun
The miracle of a vehicle
Some dancers and a drum

Road trips and red jellos along
Road trips and red jellos along

You Deserve a Better Life

The cannabis company scrubbers,
roll up our windows
against their iron-skunk emissions,

our honest boy, rising sleepyhead,
hoping there will be time
            to play before school.

Against the North End's
west wind nausea,
            open air
                        land disposal,

golden rays patting
rolled windshields
that can shatter.

Summit of Mount Purgatory

There was a time before her
when the world was charcoal grey,
when thrumming guitars were exiles
without their fiddle leads,
there was a time before her
when some of this made sense,
the poet's confusions growing
without seeds of providence.

Thumping tipper against bodhrán
like distant pounding guns,
until that blue-eyed lighting strike
and the wildness of her tongue.
Harps play to soothe his weariness
as verdant vines mature,
like Dante and Virgil's journey
through visions and fever dreams,
there was a time before her
the thresh of Purgatorio.

There was a time before
when he was half as strong,
no uillcan pipes coloured the night
and all his words were wrong,
spanking tipper against goatskin
like distant pounding guns,
before her blue-eyed lighting strike
and the wildness of her tongue.

Symmetry

Slowly removing skins
a delicate undressing
of fruits that I slice and slip
into your mouth
tracing lips with
fingers dipped in sugars
rivulets down my wrist

the last birdsong before
the nocturnal symphony tunes
straight line satellites move
across star sewn ceiling
embers trying to unite
with a miasma of fireflies
the cerise of ending light
ascension of blues and greys
a sky black licorice curtain

I will not avert
to this celestial scene above
my gaze levelled
through dancing flames
steady across our distances
received into the joyful abyss
of your eyes
dilated in our symmetry

Kitchen Table

A repurposed barn door,
sturdy as youthful shoulders,
danced upon at birthday parties,
with seven, then twelve,
and fifteen candles.

The red tablecloth is a bedspread,
your long dark hair fanned out,
our concordant rhythm,
short skirt raised
like nets for fishes,
in the ecstatic clapping
of rattling dishes.

Almost Touch

As if you were two south poles,
invisible loops of force denying
the same space, your finger,
only a cardboard fold from
the slope of your mother's eye,
almost touching her eyelash
as she drove you to school,
in singsong—would taunt,
"I'm not even touching you."

Years later, on the birthing bed,
as uterine contractions came
in mad waves, the profound
relief of a healthy daughter,
placenta-fingerpainted thighs,
with her resting, the warmth
and wet of your breast, cool
shocks of air filling her lungs,
your mother's finger moved
into your periphery, almost
touching.

Halcyon Days

Stretch lines are
watermarks, love letters
of choice and chance,
those tattered tapestries—
distant memories
in the smoky rooms of youth,
tall pines that thundered
intercourse with the sky
have surrendered
their needles as castoffs,
rough bark bleeding sap
from axe wounds,
that impetuous tattoo
—an offering
for a previous lover,
smeared like footprints
tracked through blood.

Lake

Holding one breath,
kicking and reaching down,
pulling an invisible knotted cord,
in the shadow depths,
beneath a floating dock
searching for your Claddagh ring.

There is a point when resolve
becomes suicide, when pulling arms
burn wildly like dry timber,
a piling of weight.

Hands hit silt, fingers rake,
clawing through milfoil,
desperate to exhale,
empty champagne bottles,
a rubber boot, then finding it,
frantically upward now,
kicking against the blackening,
to the precious above,
surfacing like marriage.

Eclipse

In tandem lawn chairs,
they silently read hardcover books
in the sun, a quilt tucked under arthritic legs,
wicker hats, wrinkled hands.
We had driven North,
along the shadow's path in the zone of totality,
pulled over at the white church in Rogersville
to wait roadside on our tailgate.
Slowly the moon swallowed the sun.
The ancients must have seen this eye of God—
and wondered if it was the end.
Two discs hung by an unseen wire
just out of our grasp,
a cycloptic white ring burned,
birds stilled in the instant nightfall;
sunsets bloomed, straddling the horizon.
Doffing my eclipse glasses, I admired the crowd
gazing heavenward, two woven hats
were now touching,
withered hands clasped together
in the celestial alignment of love.

Atlantic Flowers

Past the eelgrass, out to the oysters,
mud squeezes like tongues between toes,

search with footpads, tiny shuffling steps,
over smooth shells, pick a few errant stones,

innerved by the skitter of green crabs,
fill onion bags—tied

with an old skipping rope. Gather buttons,
littlenecks and razors, cherrystones,

and quahogs, take an oyster knife, open a few,
waist deep in harvest fields, no fresher catch

found by feel, opened with experienced hands,
slipped from shells, moving slowly through

her tidal estuary for hours, my brined beard
dripping with dew, from Atlantic flowers.

III. Ancaster & Upper Canada

The Kiss

Crowning the Fiddler's Green overpass like mourning doves
leaning on a bridge rail in my first tie, a salt and pepper jacket,

with the first girl. Our overwatch above the QEW, speeding
cars flashing like running salmon. Her gentle pull,

inviting, I leaned in. Pick-up tires hissing against wet pavement,
a passing horn blast: we tore apart in a guilty spasm

as if we'd been caught suffocating a patient with a pillow.
After a beat, we flowed together again, the osculating circles

pulsing like a blood pressure cuff, her pleasing tongue
was like a swizzle stick in a sling drink. At the top of her street,

when I finally said *goodnight,* we kissed goodbye for another
half hour. Then I ran; three glorious miles

in grey patent leather shoes, ankle blisters blossomed;
painful rewards into a new world of love and lust.

The Politics of Violence

The day the fox staggered into the barn
my father didn't own a gun,

his whole life, a pacifist, with no desire
to harm, or hunt, or defend with force.

At the time, I saw this as a failure of
character, as a listless boat floating

without hope of shore, hated his inability
to kill, to watch his entire barn infected,

months of quarantine, the durocs fattening
to a measure that made them a loss,

their feed exceeding pork prices,
until winter's claim, the puddles froze

like stained glass that we stomped,
slaughterhouse scene, Carracci's butchery,

hung from hooves like neckties,
neck-slit during their exasperated culling.

Costume Democracy

Our house is a black obelisk that
rises monstrous from another era,

fond memories are contortions,
a costume democracy, a lonely

quiet monastery, cloistered
reflection on wrongheaded wars.

Relationships can forge election
campaigns, steady work birthing

prosperity or pain, they are
honey gathered or bloodstained,

a ladder climbed rung by rung,
a clatter of missiles fired at once,

an opium bloom's revolution,
our country, once united, untied,

ripped, undone. If she speaks to me
now, it's with a dagger tongue.

The Murders

There are wolves in the chamber of a gun,
a requiem prayer, unspooled yellow

police line, gawking neighbours behind
window blinds, nothing like this happens here,

their doorway sickly sweet, the salty
acetone of shotgun breath.

Flowerbed edges are straight like razors,
sheared hip high barber shop boxwoods,

front door agape, her body splayed, a treacly
heap, I remember her; a parent volunteer

leaning on a rake in the long jump pit,
visiting class, on every field trip, her job

as a crown lawyer, summer in the deep end
of the Lion's Club pool, June's blistering sun,

her daughter served buttercream cupcakes,
tangy, sweet, and creamy lemon.

Public Acclaim at the Liquor Control Board of Ontario

Nervous to show my stenciled
license that gave my age as twenty,
entering the musty beer store's slick sweaty
swell of hope,
I waited, inconspicuous as a wart
in the queue of fellow boozebags.

Rattling silver wheels on slide tracks
were two lane traffic;
jangling rollers that skated empties
backward like memories,
the other birthed thundering boxes of bottles,
full promises steaming like progress.

I emerged from the LCBO to adoration,
could hear my friends cheering from the car
clear across the parking lot,
triumphant as stadium concertgoers.
Bad Company's *Feel like Makin' Love*
playing on the radio.

The Hitchhiker With a Spear

Like many stories about my father
this one begins with a horse,

a filly named Peggy who refused
to step up into her trailer,

obstinate as a Roman phalanx, fought,
kicked and rolled on the ground,

would not capitulate to her destiny.
Exhausted my father hitched her

bridal to a lead and held his arm out
the truck as we drove, I shifted the gears,

poorly, I was ten years old.
Each time I gnashed metal my father

shouted, "Fuck." When faced with oncoming
traffic we eased to the shoulder

perilously close to ditches. This fifteen
minute drive took over an hour.

Stabled the horse at the old Ancaster Fairgrounds,
returned, stopping on Southcote Road

to pick up a hitchhiker, long bearded
wearing a potato sack robe and carrying a spear

that he placed behind our cab.
He is, in all my life, the only person

I have seen carrying a spear. He smoked
a cigarette with my father, puffing and rambling

with me trapped in the middle, we were
pulled over for speeding. Incredulous,

Dad refused small talk with the officer, who
was also curious about the spear.

"Go write your fucking ticket," Dad barked.
I'm not sure what I learned that day; maybe

problem solving, the brevity of short tempered
men, tolerance, taking risks.

Most of my father's lessons were enigmatic,
this was my strange eulogy for his funeral.

The Drowning

A honey gatherer
in the cider orchards,
he was a stream surge
from overflowing spring melt,
powered the mill wheels
of embonpoint girls.
My mother was one, taken
by his flaming hair,
his sure footedness at
everything he tried,
by his comedic self-effacement.

At the tarn below
Father Loftus School,
an agile fox who could not
swim a stroke.
Pushed in by jealous suitors,
his drowning began with
unnatural yarls, awkward slaps,
they thought he was musing,

then
an
abrupt
descent.

Reverent Brown dove
so many times they had to
restrain him, spent.
Frogmen from Hamilton
were called to retrieve the body;
found tangled in fence wire,
laid him like a doll on the bray,
a pre-Raphaelite,

like Chatterton in his white shirt
and rolled jeans.

The township blamed the pond:
truckloads of fill came,
and heavy hydraulic loaders
like grave diggers
packed the basin.
My young father was there
that day, comforting a girl
reeling with guilt.
I am alive
because of a drowning.

Friends as Fingers

In the queue at Canada Post
holding the ashes of my dad
within a foam packed parcel,
the weight, the funerary box
and crushed velvet bag
was a basket of eggs,
the gentle pull of gravity like
the questioning tug of horse reins.

I remember winter woods,
stepping high over snow drifts
into my father's footprints,
and asking, "How do you know
if you have lived a successful life?"
Pulling off a buckskin work glove,
looking over his broad shoulder,
held up a naked palm,
"You know you have lived
a successful life, when
you have as many true friends
as fingers on your right hand."

He asked for a final sulky ride,
one last time around a half-mile track
behind a trotter, the two-step
dancing rhythm of hooves,
behind the creak of halter and harness,
the shooshing mud arcing from wheels,
clods flipping off shoes. A lifelong pal
driving, the urn tucked beside.
Their pace quickens in the backstretch,
the horse, blowing in joyful bursts,
comes thundering.

MONKEY
for Terri

Telephone poles with their stretching
moon shadows stripe the Radial Line,
the old tracks pulled when the electric trains
to Brantford were scuttled. Soft winds
hint of lilac, my mother, a denier
of Irish superstitions, laying marigold sprigs
over the bones of Christians,
whispering a prayer for Walter,
whose house still stands
down the old mill hill.

Down the old mill hill,

his pet monkey once tangled its thin claws
in my cousin's long hair, teeth bared,
and demon shrieked at the terrified child,
obstinately clutching knots,
had to be slowly unfurled,
removed like a burr.

A stroke left Walter's fingers crooked,
his speech drunken, drooling,
red suspender straps falling from his
once broad shoulders. And I thought getting
older to be a curse, not as inevitable,
not as some type of solid blessing
for so many days on earth.

Three children hitting a barrage
of piano keys, outside the swaying trees
titter tapping terneplate eaves, hushing leaves,
monkey screams.

Up the old mill hill, up the old mill hill,
toward the cemetery,
where I will lay beside you,
and you beside me.

Calorimetry

When lights come on, insects scatter, if your father says them,
insults matter, so leave home with a bed roll,

a flask, a flick knife that you can flash, a litany of risky nights,
hard talk, a mugging, fist fights. Christmas Dinner with an onion,

Shake 'n Bake and mayo. Heavy snow pommeled the escarpment
to blackout, no back rent, when she knocked,

stepping from lonely shadows, mixed gin with gingers,
played with string calloused fingers,

the first pressure of booze burning lips, the pleasure of hips
that prove their meaning, a line of streetlamps revived,

fluorescing above, knowing the opposite of loneliness,
within the calorimetry of love.

Brantford Serenade

The kind of joint where waitresses call you Darlin'
and Sweetie, take smoke breaks with regulars,

red leather stools punctuate Formica counters,
plump as trumpeter cheeks, coffee pours perpetual.

Is that Walter Gretzky at the end of the bench?
He scissors over the boards, long strides

across waxed tiles, circling with a puck
behind breakfast tables, unexpectedly turning

as if slipping a hip-check. Stools swivel,
and he begins to sing, taking a girl by her hands

as if warming them. Here in this roadside diner,
crooning a love song, as if happiness were a hockey

sweater, holding her with his own gentle hands
that tied so many early morning skates.

Trade Union Tire Spikes

Basement and garage armourers
manufactured them in the hundreds,

Stelco steelmen with tensile scrap metal,
lifted from cutting room floors.

Workers, linked armed strikers,
picket signs hammered down on cars,

on scabs who crossed labour gauntlets,
their tires sliced like peaches.

Celestial spikes sculpted on anvils,
steel thorns finished with wet stones,

every wound they drew was precious,
split palms, pierced ankles, four-pronged.

Trade union songs of righteous mayhem,
pin light caltrops aloft Bethlehem.

Inkwells

Dry inkwells agape
from the corners of worn desktops,
Holly Templeton waits for the poem
that I will pass like a secret.

Randy Bogle's hot flatulence
floats like a bloated body
wearing a balaclava; I sense it,
and am embarrassed for his *faux pas*.

Randy corkscrews,
I expect a muted apology,
but he points a dirty fingernail at me,
"Oh man, you're rank!" he half shouts.
"Oh Heavens, something inside you
has died. Please visit the apothecary."

Classroom laughter's clatter, Holly
hooks the stitching of her sweater over,
like a stagecoach bandit, using the pink
perfumed yarnwork as a filter.

Randy turns, leaving me to foment,
and reflect on our relationship from
second year, when he dispassionately
strung up evidence that denied
the existence of Santa.

Right now, Randy, you fart-squealer,
I should be writing
a love letter to my wife.

Ahriman

Baleful words like stone knives
gouged a thousand scars,

"It will be so easy to murder you,"
he boasts, "*when I have the guts.*"

Then kicks his own car, leaving
a concave exclamation mark.

Neighbours warn he's been watching,
parked across the street, in shadows,

backdoor exits become rehearsals,
beyond the threshold, she braces,

buttresses against paralysis,
unlatches their security chain,

escape routes are planned,
envisions her final stand, slides

the deadbolt's metallic coupling
from the frame, clicks like the action

of a gun, steps from her secure
illusion, to the far side of beyond.

Driver Safety

In the prelude
to foreplay,
she
casually mentioned
a road trip sex act
with a former lover.

Three years
into our relationship,
the odometer
has clicked off
two
hundred thousand
miles
of blowjobless
travel.

IV. The United Kingdom

The Bird and the Baby

With enough watermarks on the table to unify Mordor,
they kept the cold-boned rain from invading, hearthside,

tucked in the narrows of the Rabbit Room where Tolkien
unfurled maps of Middle-earth

and C.S. Lewis toasted the landlord's health, armloads
of prose, and an old pay window to a soldier's worth,

T.E. Lawrence with a pistol on his way to Jesus,
traded motorcycle boots for Bedouin scarves,

downwind the Martyrs' Spire, A.E. Housman with his
satchel of Shropshire verse takes pin-striped strides

across Saint Giles'. Jericho Jimmy snaps a *Big Issue*,
you can smell the Blackfriar's chimney,

there's a tall stone sundial at Corpus Christi, the lean
obelisk crowned with golden pelican, in piety,

plucks her breast in self-sacrifice, grotesques stare down
from every peak and spire, in the Ashmolean, mounds

of stolen antiquities glitter like Smaug's treasure hills.
Ages of poets and pilgrims drank here, a mythology

of elbows buttressing holy wood, long stemmed
pipes rupturing cloudy halos of imagination,

dissipating into our days, with comrades, within
these beer smudged rooms,

before our final homeward journeys, the rolling
of the scrolls, the retracing of distances.

Gloucester Green

The only public bog
on the coach platform
reached out with rancid
latrinal breath,
I pulled a shemagh
over my face to blunt it.
My friend of a thousand miles
standing queue
for our olive drab duffels.
The washroom stalls
gawked, without doors,
absent toilet seats.
Depictions of devilry
and descent scarred the walls,
the first bowl eviscerated excrement
like Dante's eighth circle,
ready to immerse the flatterers.

I journeyed deeper;
in the middle frame
a man was thrusting into a woman
whose leather skirt was hiked up
like a wind torn umbrella.
The last panel, the subject—
a miserable boy, Jean Valjean
with a yellow passport,
wearing an oversize jacket
and striped school tie.
"I giff da besht blowy
in Oxordshire," he said,
"cush I gotch nar teesh,"
demonstrated with a fist,
a wry toothless smile,
dilated sapphire-green eyes.
"Only five poundsh mate."

My friend of a thousand miles
asked how the shitters looked.
"Go to the third stall," I advised,
"for aesthetic rapture."
Returning quickly,
called me an asshole.

My Grandfather Played the Violin

While excavating the trainline
they unearthed a Roman ring.
One railway man, killed on the job,
is buried here under a fading poem,
slowly eroding from limestone.
At the back of the congregation
the choir sings *Be Not Afraid*,
an elderly woman turns.

Bellringers play a peal of six
with ropes, then drift like fog
though the cemetery bounds
onto Sheep Street,
the churchyard is absent a fence,
its wrought iron requisitioned
as salvage, repurposed
for munitions during the war.

They wander like shepherds
toward the cobblestone glow
of the pub, to pints and passions
inside The Rose and Crown.
Nine-hundred-year-old walls,
honey-yellowed Cotswold stone
planted over the bones
of a Saxon ruin.

Shuffling through the Narthex,
wearing a handsewn pattern dress
and a string of pearls, corkscrews
at her pew,
turns, with cloudy eyes fixed,
tiny sliding steps,
hand over hand along the rails.

Smiles as if seeing a lover,
takes my arm for balance,
asks me if I am Canadian,
if my grandfather was a soldier,
and did he play the fiddle.

Gender Politics

A slattern drowning, still wearing the linen
shawl she was murdered in, now a tattering.

The dead witch, kept from rising, a scythe
across her throat rusting with the seasons,

a shroud exhumed; her corpse desiccated.
The skeletal toe bone padlocked like a wedding

ring—marriage vows with her executioners.
Suspicious cross-eyed women, a Devil's gap

between their teeth—slip a serpent's tongue,
en garde of a pert breast or murderers' thumbs.

Other dark markers; heterochromia, gazing
lustfully toward pay equity, or women fighting

for a bench in parliament, arguing in the
boardrooms, for dominance in their bedrooms,

for control of their bodies; these cunning,
misaligned consorts of postmodernity.

My Poet Friend

You are not a pizza,
you are a poem,
you are free jazz
with a bright melody
then a sudden full stop.
You're percussion and illumination,
you're the cherry on top,
and the pistol
cocked and locked.

Literary Criticism

Rat claw scratches
over my first drafts,

She edits at the pub,
laughs when she loathes

a poem, folds the page
slowly, marks the crease

with a lipstick seal,
her attitude's stigma.

I call for the cheque,
brusquely drive home,

make love roughly
on our front stairwell,

clothes shed to fight,
slip our tongues over

each turn of phrase, to get
the enjambment right.

Job Interview From the Rose & Crown, Charlbury Oxon

The panel of four School Principals
assembled like a Court Martial.

I found myself in The Rose & Crown,
making friends with the publican who

agreed to loan me his telephone.
A discrepancy with the time change

between Canada and England
resulted in the taking of a pint,

or several braces before the call came.
I'd become wassailed enough to slip

down a waterslide.
The peat hearth's pulsing heat

broke me into a lover's sudor.
Our black-haired barmaid shushed locals

who crowded too close. I began laughing
with inanity, quickly reeled it in,

over pronouncing words
to avoid sodden tumbles,

ignoring whispered advice of gawkers,
drinking the moment to its lees,

ended the interview to barroom cheers,
I've been teaching for twenty years.

V. The End

Goodbye

The characters I created became old friends,
The Claw and his brother, experts of tickle torture;

Bob and Sob, who chant about corn-on-the-cob,
identical twin fists with thumbs for mouths.

Beneath blankets under bedsheets,
an Irish cave dweller, Darby Underhill,

always ready to sing *The Old Triangle*,
armed with a trusty blackthorn shillelagh.

Yesterday, Finley, now eight years old,
called them all out;

I became their busy puppeteer with voices
and a Belfast accent.

He thanked them for years of bedtime play,
but now was too mature, said he loved them all,

kissed my hands as if they were soldiers
heading to war, and whispered goodbye.

So unexpected, a tear fell. Papa, he asked,
are you going to miss them too?

Metaphysical Question

In *Kespek* they ask, *Tami Tleawin*?
Denis answers his own question,

Win winibeske,
"My people come from,"

decodes the literal meaning, the shadow
of those who came before.

The great burning fire reveals them,
so you can see your forebears follow.

He has a brother, not of blood, who comes
flitting like a sparrow to his home

as he pleases. He too, will become
part of their ancestral penumbra.

My little boy, wide and wounded
from news, the growing realization

that our time with her narrows, the disease,
whose name we never say, moves

like blister rust over white pine. When he asks,
When Momma dies, where will she go?

Maybe I will tell him, behind every footfall,
she will be there, forever as your shadow.

On Losing a War

The empty four-square court, discarded jump rope
dangling from a rusting Russian tank, back home

maple keys reverse pirouette to Tarvia like auto
gyrating helicopters, separated seedpods

pressed on Ikram's nose, a schoolyard rhinoceros
at the ellipse of a season.

One plastic soldier with a drooping rifle, forgotten
in the sandbox, his country fatigued,

fourteen years of war that has come to nothing.
This tribal landscape swallowed another army,

bled them out on harsh hallowed ground.
Afghan girls now forbidden from schools,

women's voices no longer sing, even learning
becomes a crime. The Taliban warned

"Canadians will wear their watches,
but we have all the time."

I'll Take a Short Death Please

To be shot
in the back of the head
by a jealous husband,
a javelin to the temple
thrown by Agamemnon,
cleave my throat Achilles,
then drag my broken bones
around the walls of Ilium.

Gainsay their long walk
to the clumsy gallows,
I don't want to see Death
riding a camel across
the desert for days.

Let the last time
serve as goodbye,
the last we loved, linger
like the smell of each other,
and one final darling kiss
to become a poem
pressed between pages.

Donnie Is Coming For Sure

Helmet scrim and webbing, recce team
orienting the director-stand, Prairie rain,
polished glass boot-caps in barracks,
and caring for the darling screw-guns
of the field artillery.

Met a wheat-haired girl in the smoky
barrooms of Edmonton,
left mud-gunning and deployments
for the safety of a union job in PEI,
away from cordite explosives,
rucksack marches,
feral combat zones,
his pregnant wife, home, holding
together strands with both hands,
weaving their Nativity tapestry,
swaddling the baby for a journey.

He went ahead a fortnight to start
that new job,
"One last reconnaissance,
to prepare their homecoming."
His wife and newborn were in flight
when Donnie was killed, boot-slip
under an asphalt compactor.

His parents, having never met their
grandson or daughter-in-law,
wailed
and waited,
standing fire picket
in Terminal Arrivals,
her name on a placard.

After a long season,
when autumn had finally undressed
the Darnley Road, woodlands ready
to make love to winter,
she packed two bags,
following the setting sun.

Lifeline

Dilaudid dilated eyes were drops of dead oil,
came slouching, that small scowl matching his height,

topped with a Toronto ball-hat with a razor-straight peak,
never looked up at the offer to share my lunch,

hissed, "Yeah I'm hungry." When I glanced next
had a mouthful of fudge, the manducated sandwich

mutilated across the desk like a murder scene,
was running the apple through with a broken pencil.

"What are you doing?" I asked, unveiling disgust.
He held it up like a head on a pike, "You want it asshole?"

I yanked it off the stave and took a bite, smugly staring
a challenge, chewing slowly until he had to look away,

kicked over a chair and was gone. An hour later,
facial features compressed in a stocking,

robbed a gas bar at gunpoint, shed his disguise
within range of the security camera.

But he came to school that day.
Drowning, yet I refused to pitch the buoy line.

Crematoria III

That time in Krakov when we took the
train to Auschwitz, in the latrine you

could smell a supernatural manifestation,
rooms of human hair for darning socks,

tiny buckles and red shoes, the birds,
silent voyeurs perched on gallows,

then into gas chamber where
pyramids of souls were consumed,

staring up into the murder hole
for Zyklon-B cannisters,

the stolen possessions, their most precious
personal treasures, sorted in warehouses

Kanada 1 and Kanada 2, because
Canada seemed a land of everything.

Petr Eisler's suitcase haunts me, little
annihilated boy, so do the nail scratches

on walls, the wrought iron warning,
the electrified fences,

the liars and deniers who make
the last gasps of a million souls

not worth an ounce of spit, the tight
little prayers pushed into a thermos flask

and buried in the ashpit of history.
So many lost poets and painters,

lives, extinguished, stolen from the
world, in the violence of indifference,

that threatens every time we remain
silent, when we ought to start gouging.

When I Die

Play *The Power of Love* at the funeral,
Craig will strip his shirt and dance
bare chested in one of my striped ties,
that rhythmic prance and hip shake
he calls *Le Renard*, Handsome
Mark Sampson should sing my eulogy,
wipe my wife's tears if any, or many,
Colonel Finley Mullally will subtract
a sugar scoop of ash, grey dust
that used to be my body,
divide me between a battery of guns,
fire me from the howitzers
to drift with cordite smoke
during a ceremonial salute,
says he will put in enough ash
to coat the faces of gawkers,
at a celebration to honour our King,
or sombre remembrance,
at the next occasion, crashing
one last glorious party
that I was not invited to.

The Fourth Wall

My friend scissored over the centenary railing,
handcuffed himself to a waist harness,

backpack bulging with boxes of finishing nails,
drowning himself in river waters, cold.

Stumbled over these grisly details a year after
his funeral, absent the evolution of grief.

Days are a laminar flow, unrecognizable,
an illusion of stillness—but pouring forth.

I know you understand how these stutter steps,
sudden stair trips, aren't always obvious.

By the time you read this offering
my tallow candle drips, lifetimes unfold

like stanzas—a *memento mori*. We are passing
over lines that merge into our story

until this meeting ends, and, even if we haven't
kept company in person, I consider you a friend.

So Dear Reader, I am pricking this final pomander,
patterns of calyx for every year I have dreamed

and breathed clove scented days. I too will park
before the Caledonia Bridge, wipe snow from

steel palings, four-ways blinking, keys tucked
into the column, wallet yawning on the dashboard,

over the handrail of this last forlorn verse, curse,
and leap from and return to—this beautiful earth.

Acknowledgements

My heartfelt thanks to teachers. I've been lucky enough to have a few that changed the arc of my life—namely Professor Bob Spree, Coach Wayne Hager, and Dr. Douglas Mantz.

Thank you, Chris Needham, my editor, and NON Publishing for giving me a chance three books ago.

There's no way I can properly thank Handsome Mark Sampson for all his work editing and helping me rewrite, revise, and sometimes wheelbarrow my poems to the manure pile. Mark kept me punching even when I was a standing knockout, the best cornerman with a stool and the cut jelly. I love you brother.

Cheers to Andrew LaFleche and Terri Beckwith for editorial assistance.

Thanks to all the fine folks at The Northrop Frye International Literary Festival and the Writers' Federation of New Brunswick for the opportunities to share my work.

I am blessed for Finley, Corrine, and Terri.